Pascale Leconte

The little book of **Mantras** to be whispered

Translated from the French: Laurent Thompson.
Cover: Hannah Edgman from Pixabay.com

© 2020, Pascale Leconte
Edition : Books on Demand,
12/14 rond-Point des Champs-Elysées, 75008 Paris
Impression : BoD - Books on Demand, Norderstedt, Allemagne
ISBN : 9782322222698
Dépôt légal : Mai 2020

I am boundless. Everything is possible. I am boundless.

I am perfect. I am perfect.

I listen to my joy. It's my inner compass. I listen to my joy. It's my inner compass.

Time is an illusion. Time is an illusion.

I love myself unconditionally. I love myself unconditionally.

Only Love exists. Only Love exists.

This world of duality is an illusion. This world of duality is an illusion.

In presence. In presence.

I am. I'm. I am. I'm. I am. I'm. I am. I'm.
I am. I'm. I am. I'm. I am. I'm. I am. I'm. I am. I'm.
I am. I'm. I am. I'm. I am. I'm. I am. I'm. I am. I'm.
I am. I'm. I am. I'm. I am. I'm. I am. I'm. I am. I'm.
I am. I'm. I am. I'm. I am. I'm. I am. I'm. I am. I'm.
I am. I'm. I am. I'm. I am. I'm. I am. I'm. I am. I'm.
I am. I'm. I am. I'm. I am. I'm. I am. I'm. I am. I'm.
I am. I'm. I am. I'm. I am. I'm. I am. I'm. I am. I'm.
I am. I'm. I am. I'm. I am. I'm. I am. I'm. I am. I'm.
I am. I'm. I am. I'm. I am. I'm. I am. I'm. I am. I'm.
I am. I'm. I am. I'm. I am. I'm. I am. I'm. I am. I'm.
I am. I'm. I am. I'm. I am. I'm. I am. I'm. I am. I'm.
I am. I'm. I am. I'm. I am. I'm. I am. I'm. I am. I'm.
I am. I'm. I am. I'm. I am. I'm. I am. I'm. I am. I'm.
I am. I'm. I am. I'm. I am. I'm. I am. I'm. I am. I'm.
I am. I'm. I am. I'm. I am. I'm. I am. I'm. I am. I'm.
I am. I'm. I am. I'm. I am. I'm. I am. I'm. I am. I'm.
I am. I'm. I am. I'm. I am. I'm. I am. I'm. I am. I'm.
I am. I'm. I am. I'm. I am. I'm. I am. I'm. I am. I'm.
I am. I'm. I am. I'm. I am. I'm. I am. I'm. I am. I'm.
I am. I'm. I am. I'm. I am. I'm. I am. I'm. I am. I'm.
I am. I'm. I am. I'm. I am. I'm. I am. I'm. I am. I'm.
I am. I'm. I am. I'm. I am. I'm. I am. I'm. I am. I'm.
I am. I'm. I am. I'm. I am. I'm. I am. I'm. I am. I'm.
I am. I'm. I am. I'm. I am. I'm. I am. I'm. I am. I'm.
I am. I'm. I am. I'm. I am. I'm. I am. I'm. I am. I'm.
I am. I'm. I am. I'm. I am. I'm. I am. I'm. I am. I'm.
I am. I'm. I am. I'm. I am. I'm. I am. I'm. I am. I'm.
I am. I'm. I am. I'm. I am. I'm. I am. I'm. I am. I'm.
I am. I'm. I am. I'm. I am. I'm. I am. I'm. I am. I'm.

Everything is ONE. Everything is ONE.

I am complete. I don't need anything nor anybody. I am complete. I don't need anything nor anybody.

Everything is already accomplished. Everything is already accomplished.

Nothing is important. Nothing is important.

The only reason for being is loving. TO LOVE. To love everything and everybody, starting by loving myself. The only reason for being is loving. TO LOVE. To love everything and everybody, starting by loving myself. The only reason for being is loving. TO LOVE. To love everything and everybody, starting by loving myself. The only reason for being is loving. TO LOVE. To love everything and everybody, starting by loving myself. The only reason for being is loving. TO LOVE. To love everything and everybody, starting by loving myself. The only reason for being is loving. TO LOVE. To love everything and everybody, starting by loving myself. The only reason for being is loving. TO LOVE. To love everything and everybody, starting by loving myself. The only reason for being is loving. TO LOVE. To love everything and everybody, starting by loving myself. The only reason for being is loving. TO LOVE. To love everything and everybody, starting by loving myself. The only reason for being is loving. TO LOVE. To love everything and everybody, starting by loving myself. The only reason for being is loving. TO LOVE. To love everything and everybody, starting by loving myself. The only reason for being is loving. TO LOVE. To love everything and everybody, starting by loving myself. The only reason for being is loving. TO LOVE. To love everything and everybody, starting by loving myself. The only reason for being is loving. TO LOVE.

I respect myself. I respect my body. I respect my limits. I respect my decisions. I respect myself. I respect my body. I respect my limits. I respect my decisions. I respect myself. I respect my body. I respect my limits. I respect my decisions. I respect myself. I respect my body. I respect my limits. I respect my decisions. I respect myself. I respect my body. I respect my limits. I respect my decisions. I respect myself. I respect my body. I respect my limits. I respect my decisions. I respect myself. I respect my body. I respect my limits. I respect my decisions. I respect myself. I respect my body. I respect my limits. I respect my decisions. I respect myself. I respect my body. I respect my limits. I respect my decisions. I respect myself. I respect my body. I respect my limits. I respect my decisions. I respect myself. I respect my body. I respect my limits. I respect my decisions. I respect myself. I respect my body. I respect my limits. I respect my decisions. I respect myself. I respect my body. I respect my limits. I respect my decisions. I respect myself. I respect my body. I respect my limits. I respect my decisions. I respect myself. I respect my body. I respect my limits. I respect my decisions. I respect myself. I respect my body. I respect my limits. I respect my decisions.

What would Love do in my situation? What would Love do in my situation?

Thoughts pass through me, but I am not them nor are they me. Thoughts pass through me, but I am not them nor are they me.

I am ALL. I am ALL. I am ALL. I am ALL.
I am ALL. I am ALL. I am ALL. I am ALL. I am
ALL. I am ALL. I am ALL. I am ALL. I am ALL.
I am ALL. I am ALL. I am ALL. I am ALL. I am
ALL. I am ALL. I am ALL. I am ALL. I am ALL.
I am ALL. I am ALL. I am ALL. I am ALL. I am
ALL. I am ALL. I am ALL. I am ALL. I am ALL.
I am ALL. I am ALL. I am ALL. I am ALL. I am
ALL. I am ALL. I am ALL. I am ALL. I am ALL.
I am ALL. I am ALL. I am ALL. I am ALL. I am
ALL. I am ALL. I am ALL. I am ALL. I am ALL.
I am ALL. I am ALL. I am ALL. I am ALL. I am
ALL. I am ALL. I am ALL. I am ALL. I am ALL.
I am ALL. I am ALL. I am ALL. I am ALL. I am
ALL. I am ALL. I am ALL. I am ALL. I am ALL.
I am ALL. I am ALL. I am ALL. I am ALL. I am
ALL. I am ALL. I am ALL. I am ALL. I am ALL.
I am ALL. I am ALL. I am ALL. I am ALL. I am
ALL. I am ALL. I am ALL. I am ALL. I am ALL.
I am ALL. I am ALL. I am ALL. I am ALL. I am
ALL. I am ALL. I am ALL. I am ALL. I am ALL.
I am ALL. I am ALL. I am ALL. I am ALL. I am
ALL. I am ALL. I am ALL. I am ALL. I am ALL.
I am ALL. I am ALL. I am ALL. I am ALL. I am
ALL. I am ALL. I am ALL. I am ALL. I am ALL.
I am ALL. I am ALL. I am ALL. I am ALL. I am
ALL. I am ALL. I am ALL. I am ALL. I am ALL.
I am ALL. I am ALL. I am ALL. I am ALL.

Here and now. Here and now.

Duality begins with 'I'. ONE. UNITY. Duality begins with 'I'. ONE. UNITY.

I am loved. I am loved.

I am pure Love. I am pure Love.

I'm sorry. Forgive me. Thank you. I love you. I'm sorry. Forgive me. Thank you. I love you.

I'm sorry. I forgive myself. I thank myself. I love myself. I'm sorry. I forgive myself. I thank myself. I love myself.

We are all connected. If I evolve, everything evolves. If I evolve, Humanity evolves. If I evolve, the Universe evolves. We are all connected. If I evolve, everything evolves. If I evolve, Humanity evolves. If I evolve, the Universe evolves. We are all connected. If I evolve, everything evolves. If I evolve, Humanity evolves. If I evolve, the Universe evolves. We are all connected. If I evolve, everything evolves. If I evolve, Humanity evolves. If I evolve, the Universe evolves. We are all connected. If I evolve, everything evolves. If I evolve, Humanity evolves. If I evolve, the Universe evolves. We are all connected. If I evolve, everything evolves. If I evolve, Humanity evolves. If I evolve, the Universe evolves. We are all connected. If I evolve, everything evolves. If I evolve, Humanity evolves. If I evolve, the Universe evolves. We are all connected. If I evolve, everything evolves. If I evolve, Humanity evolves. If I evolve, the Universe evolves. We are all connected. If I evolve, everything evolves. If I evolve, Humanity evolves. If I evolve, the Universe evolves. We are all connected. If I evolve, everything evolves. If I evolve, Humanity evolves. If I evolve, the Universe evolves. We are all connected. If I evolve, everything evolves. If I evolve, Humanity evolves. If I evolve, the Universe evolves.

Everything is perfect. Everything is perfect.
Everything is perfect. Everything is perfect.
Everything is perfect. Everything is perfect.
Everything is perfect. Everything is perfect.
Everything is perfect. Everything is perfect.
Everything is perfect. Everything is perfect.
Everything is perfect. Everything is perfect.
Everything is perfect. Everything is perfect.
Everything is perfect. Everything is perfect.
Everything is perfect. Everything is perfect.
Everything is perfect. Everything is perfect.
Everything is perfect. Everything is perfect.
Everything is perfect. Everything is perfect.
Everything is perfect. Everything is perfect.
Everything is perfect. Everything is perfect.
Everything is perfect. Everything is perfect.
Everything is perfect. Everything is perfect.
Everything is perfect. Everything is perfect.
Everything is perfect. Everything is perfect.
Everything is perfect. Everything is perfect.
Everything is perfect. Everything is perfect.
Everything is perfect. Everything is perfect.
Everything is perfect. Everything is perfect.
Everything is perfect. Everything is perfect.
Everything is perfect. Everything is perfect.
Everything is perfect. Everything is perfect.
Everything is perfect. Everything is perfect.
Everything is perfect. Everything is perfect.
Everything is perfect. Everything is perfect.
Everything is perfect. Everything is perfect.
Everything is perfect. Everything is perfect.
Everything is perfect.

I welcome my fear. I love my fear. I welcome my fear. I love my fear.

Now. Now. Now. Now. Now. Now. Now.
Now. Now. Now. Now. Now. Now. Now. Now.
Now. Now. Now. Now. Now. Now. Now. Now.
Now. Now. Now. Now. Now. Now. Now. Now.
Now. Now. Now. Now. Now. Now. Now. Now.
Now. Now. Now. Now. Now. Now. Now. Now.
Now. Now. Now. Now. Now. Now. Now. Now.
Now. Now. Now. Now. Now. Now. Now. Now.
Now. Now. Now. Now. Now. Now. Now. Now.
Now. Now. Now. Now. Now. Now. Now. Now.
Now. Now. Now. Now. Now. Now. Now. Now.
Now. Now. Now. Now. Now. Now. Now. Now.
Now. Now. Now. Now. Now. Now. Now. Now.
Now. Now. Now. Now. Now. Now. Now. Now.
Now. Now. Now. Now. Now. Now. Now. Now.
Now. Now. Now. Now. Now. Now. Now. Now.
Now. Now. Now. Now. Now. Now. Now. Now.
Now. Now. Now. Now. Now. Now. Now. Now.
Now. Now. Now. Now. Now. Now. Now. Now.
Now. Now. Now. Now. Now. Now. Now. Now.
Now. Now. Now. Now. Now. Now. Now. Now.
Now. Now. Now. Now. Now. Now. Now. Now.
Now. Now. Now. Now. Now. Now. Now. Now.
Now. Now. Now. Now. Now. Now. Now. Now.
Now. Now. Now. Now. Now. Now. Now. Now.
Now. Now. Now. Now. Now. Now. Now. Now.
Now. Now. Now. Now. Now. Now. Now. Now.
Now. Now. Now. Now. Now. Now. Now. Now.
Now. Now. Now. Now. Now. Now. Now. Now.
Now. Now. Now. Now. Now. Now. Now. Now.
Now.

Fear doesn't exist. Love is ALL. Fear doesn't exist. Love is ALL.

Unity is changeless truth. Unity is changeless truth.

Good and evil are two sides of the same coin. This coin is me. This coin is EVERYTHING. Good and evil are two sides of the same coin. This coin is me. This coin is EVERYTHING. Good and evil are two sides of the same coin. This coin is me. This coin is EVERYTHING. Good and evil are two sides of the same coin. This coin is me. This coin is EVERYTHING. Good and evil are two sides of the same coin. This coin is me. This coin is EVERYTHING. Good and evil are two sides of the same coin. This coin is me. This coin is EVERYTHING. Good and evil are two sides of the same coin. This coin is me. This coin is EVERYTHING. Good and evil are two sides of the same coin. This coin is me. This coin is EVERYTHING. Good and evil are two sides of the same coin. This coin is me. This coin is EVERYTHING. Good and evil are two sides of the same coin. This coin is me. This coin is EVERYTHING. Good and evil are two sides of the same coin. This coin is me. This coin is EVERYTHING. Good and evil are two sides of the same coin. This coin is me. This coin is EVERYTHING. Good and evil are two sides of the same coin. This coin is me. This coin is EVERYTHING. Good and evil are two sides of the same coin. This coin is me. This coin is EVERYTHING. Good and evil are two sides of the same coin. This coin is me. This coin is EVERYTHING.

I welcome my dark sides. I love them. I shed light and Love on them. I welcome my dark sides. I love them. I shed light and Love on them. I welcome my dark sides. I love them. I shed light and Love on them. I welcome my dark sides. I love them. I shed light and Love on them. I welcome my dark sides. I love them. I shed light and Love on them. I welcome my dark sides. I love them. I shed light and Love on them. I welcome my dark sides. I love them. I shed light and Love on them. I welcome my dark sides. I love them. I shed light and Love on them. I welcome my dark sides. I love them. I shed light and Love on them. I welcome my dark sides. I love them. I shed light and Love on them. I welcome my dark sides. I love them. I shed light and Love on them. I welcome my dark sides. I love them. I shed light and Love on them. I welcome my dark sides. I love them. I shed light and Love on them. I welcome my dark sides. I love them. I shed light and Love on them. I welcome my dark sides. I love them. I shed light and Love on them. I welcome my dark sides. I love them. I shed light and Love on them. I welcome my dark sides. I love them. I shed light and Love on them. I welcome my dark sides. I love them. I shed light and Love on them. I welcome my dark sides. I love them. I shed light and Love on them.

I don't judge myself. I don't judge others. I don't judge myself. I don't judge others.

I lay my attention to my body. Here and now. I follow my breath. I slow my breathing. I inhale slowly and deeply. Everything is perfect. I lay my attention to my body. Here and now. I follow my breath. I slow my breathing. I inhale slowly and deeply. Everything is perfect. I lay my attention to my body. Here and now. I follow my breath. I slow my breathing. I inhale slowly and deeply. Everything is perfect. I lay my attention to my body. Here and now. I follow my breath. I slow my breathing. I inhale slowly and deeply. Everything is perfect. I lay my attention to my body. Here and now. I follow my breath. I slow my breathing. I inhale slowly and deeply. Everything is perfect. I lay my attention to my body. Here and now. I follow my breath. I slow my breathing. I inhale slowly and deeply. Everything is perfect. I lay my attention to my body. Here and now. I follow my breath. I slow my breathing. I inhale slowly and deeply. Everything is perfect. I lay my attention to my body. Here and now. I follow my breath. I slow my breathing. I inhale slowly and deeply. Everything is perfect. I lay my attention to my body. Here and now. I follow my breath. I slow my breathing. I inhale slowly and deeply. Everything is perfect. I lay my attention to my body. Here and now. I follow my breath. I slow my breathing. I inhale slowly and deeply. Everything is perfect. I lay my attention to my body. Here and now.

Whether I love him or hate him, I am he. He is me. Whether I love him or hate him, I am he. He is me.

Every experience is learning. Every experience is learning.

Everything is experience. I congratulate myself for learning each day. Everything is experience. I congratulate myself for learning each day. Everything is experience. I congratulate myself for learning each day. Everything is experience. I congratulate myself for learning each day. Everything is experience. I congratulate myself for learning each day. Everything is experience. I congratulate myself for learning each day. Everything is experience. I congratulate myself for learning each day. Everything is experience. I congratulate myself for learning each day. Everything is experience. I congratulate myself for learning each day. Everything is experience. I congratulate myself for learning each day. Everything is experience. I congratulate myself for learning each day. Everything is experience. I congratulate myself for learning each day. Everything is experience. I congratulate myself for learning each day. Everything is experience. I congratulate myself for learning each day. Everything is experience. I congratulate myself for learning each day. Everything is experience. I congratulate myself for learning each day. Everything is experience. I congratulate myself for learning each day. Everything is experience. I congratulate myself for learning each day.

Not good nor evil. Everything is experience. Not good nor evil. Everything is experience.

I welcome my emotion benevolently. It carries a message for me. I don't reject it. I welcome my emotion benevolently. It carries a message for me. I don't reject it. I welcome my emotion benevolently. It carries a message for me. I don't reject it. I welcome my emotion benevolently. It carries a message for me. I don't reject it. I welcome my emotion benevolently. It carries a message for me. I don't reject it. I welcome my emotion benevolently. It carries a message for me. I don't reject it. I welcome my emotion benevolently. It carries a message for me. I don't reject it. I welcome my emotion benevolently. It carries a message for me. I don't reject it. I welcome my emotion benevolently. It carries a message for me. I don't reject it. I welcome my emotion benevolently. It carries a message for me. I don't reject it. I welcome my emotion benevolently. It carries a message for me. I don't reject it. I welcome my emotion benevolently. It carries a message for me. I don't reject it. I welcome my emotion benevolently. It carries a message for me. I don't reject it. I welcome my emotion benevolently. It carries a message for me. I don't reject it. I welcome my emotion benevolently. It carries a message for me. I don't reject it. I welcome my emotion benevolently. It carries a message for me. I don't reject it. I welcome my emotion benevolently. It carries a message for me. I don't reject it.

I love myself such as I am. I love myself such as I am.

I love this world such as it is. I love this world such as it is.

I love humanity such as it is. I love humanity such as it is.

I welcome this event such as it is. I welcome this event such as it is.

I don't have any expectations. Everything is already there. I don't have any expectations. Everything is already there.

I am Unconditional Love. I am Unconditional Love.

Peace is inside of me. Not outside. My joy is within me. It exists without a reason. Without a cause. Peace is inside of me. Not outside. My joy is within me. It exists without a reason. Without a cause. Peace is inside of me. Not outside. My joy is within me. It exists without a reason. Without a cause. Peace is inside of me. Not outside. My joy is within me. It exists without a reason. Without a cause. Peace is inside of me. Not outside. My joy is within me. It exists without a reason. Without a cause. Peace is inside of me. Not outside. My joy is within me. It exists without a reason. Without a cause. Peace is inside of me. Not outside. My joy is within me. It exists without a reason. Without a cause. Peace is inside of me. Not outside. My joy is within me. It exists without a reason. Without a cause. Peace is inside of me. Not outside. My joy is within me. It exists without a reason. Without a cause. Peace is inside of me. Not outside. My joy is within me. It exists without a reason. Without a cause. Peace is inside of me. Not outside. My joy is within me. It exists without a reason. Without a cause. Peace is inside of me. Not outside. My joy is within me. It exists without a reason. Without a cause. Peace is inside of me. Not outside. My joy is within me. It exists without a reason. Without a cause. Peace is inside of me. Not outside. My joy is within me. It exists without a reason. Without a cause. Peace is inside of me. Not outside. My joy is within me. It exists without a reason. Without a cause. Peace is inside of me. Not outside.

I am ageless. Time is a delusion. I am ageless. Time is a delusion.

I am sovereign over my own life. I let go of the lives of others. I am sovereign over my own life. I let go of the lives of others. I am sovereign over my own life. I let go of the lives of others. I am sovereign over my own life. I let go of the lives of others. I am sovereign over my own life. I let go of the lives of others. I am sovereign over my own life. I let go of the lives of others. I am sovereign over my own life. I let go of the lives of others. I am sovereign over my own life. I let go of the lives of others. I am sovereign over my own life. I let go of the lives of others. I am sovereign over my own life. I let go of the lives of others. I am sovereign over my own life. I let go of the lives of others. I am sovereign over my own life. I let go of the lives of others. I am sovereign over my own life. I let go of the lives of others. I am sovereign over my own life. I let go of the lives of others. I am sovereign over my own life. I let go of the lives of others. I am sovereign over my own life. I let go of the lives of others. I am sovereign over my own life. I let go of the lives of others. I am sovereign over my own life. I let go of the lives of others. I am sovereign over my own life. I let go of the lives of others. I am sovereign over my own life. I let go of the lives of others. I am sovereign over my own life. I let go of the lives of others. I am sovereign over my own life. I let go of the lives of others. I am sovereign over my own life. I let go of the lives of others. I am sovereign over my own life.

I observe the emotions running through me. I am not those emotions. They just pass through me. I observe the emotions running through me. I am not those emotions. They just pass through me. I observe the emotions running through me. I am not those emotions. They just pass through me. I observe the emotions running through me. I am not those emotions. They just pass through me. I observe the emotions running through me. I am not those emotions. They just pass through me. I observe the emotions running through me. I am not those emotions. They just pass through me. I observe the emotions running through me. I am not those emotions. They just pass through me. I observe the emotions running through me. I am not those emotions. They just pass through me. I observe the emotions running through me. I am not those emotions. They just pass through me. I observe the emotions running through me. I am not those emotions. They just pass through me. I observe the emotions running through me. I am not those emotions. They just pass through me. I observe the emotions running through me. I am not those emotions. They just pass through me. I observe the emotions running through me. I am not those emotions. They just pass through me. I observe the emotions running through me. I am not those emotions. They just pass through me. I observe the emotions running through me. I am not those emotions. They just pass through me.

I am not this incarnated person. I am ALL. I am Conscience. I am not this incarnated person. I am ALL. I am Conscience.

Only the Present counts. Only this Instant counts. Only the Present counts. Only this Instant counts.

Every judgment judges and lies. I welcome what is because everything is perfect. Every judgment judges and lies. I welcome what is because everything is perfect. Every judgment judges and lies. I welcome what is because everything is perfect. Every judgment judges and lies. I welcome what is because everything is perfect. Every judgment judges and lies. I welcome what is because everything is perfect. Every judgment judges and lies. I welcome what is because everything is perfect. Every judgment judges and lies. I welcome what is because everything is perfect. Every judgment judges and lies. I welcome what is because everything is perfect. Every judgment judges and lies. I welcome what is because everything is perfect. Every judgment judges and lies. I welcome what is because everything is perfect. Every judgment judges and lies. I welcome what is because everything is perfect. Every judgment judges and lies. I welcome what is because everything is perfect. Every judgment judges and lies. I welcome what is because everything is perfect. Every judgment judges and lies. I welcome what is because everything is perfect. Every judgment judges and lies. I welcome what is because everything is perfect. Every judgment judges and lies. I welcome what is because everything is perfect. Every judgment judges and lies. I welcome what is because everything is perfect.

Joy is my only guide. I am my joy because I am incarnate joy. Joy is my only guide.

The future doesn't exist. Only the present counts. The future doesn't exist. Only the present counts.

The past no longer exists. Only the present matters. The past no longer exists. Only the present matters.

I treat myself with Love. I treat myself with Love.

Unconditional Love. Unconditional Love.
Unconditional Love. Unconditional Love.
Unconditional Love. Unconditional Love.
Unconditional Love. Unconditional Love.
Unconditional Love. Unconditional Love.
Unconditional Love. Unconditional Love.
Unconditional Love. Unconditional Love.
Unconditional Love. Unconditional Love.
Unconditional Love. Unconditional Love.
Unconditional Love. Unconditional Love.
Unconditional Love. Unconditional Love.
Unconditional Love. Unconditional Love.
Unconditional Love. Unconditional Love.
Unconditional Love. Unconditional Love.
Unconditional Love. Unconditional Love.
Unconditional Love. Unconditional Love.
Unconditional Love. Unconditional Love.
Unconditional Love. Unconditional Love.
Unconditional Love. Unconditional Love.
Unconditional Love. Unconditional Love.
Unconditional Love. Unconditional Love.
Unconditional Love. Unconditional Love.
Unconditional Love. Unconditional Love.
Unconditional Love. Unconditional Love.
Unconditional Love. Unconditional Love.
Unconditional Love. Unconditional Love.
Unconditional Love. Unconditional Love.
Unconditional Love. Unconditional Love.
Unconditional Love. Unconditional Love.
Unconditional Love. Unconditional Love.
Unconditional Love. Unconditional Love.
Unconditional Love. Unconditional Love.
Unconditional Love.

No beginning nor end. Everything is Here and Now. No beginning nor end. Everything is Here and Now. No beginning nor end. Everything is Here and Now. No beginning nor end. Everything is Here and Now. No beginning nor end. Everything is Here and Now. No beginning nor end. Everything is Here and Now. No beginning nor end. Everything is Here and Now. No beginning nor end. Everything is Here and Now No beginning nor end. Everything is Here and Now. No beginning nor end. Everything is Here and Now. No beginning nor end. Everything is Here and Now. No beginning nor end. Everything is Here and Now. No beginning nor end. Everything is Here and Now. No beginning nor end. Everything is Here and Now. No beginning nor end. Everything is Here and Now. No beginning nor end. Everything is Here and Now. No beginning nor end. Everything is Here and Now. No beginning nor end. Everything is Here and Now. No beginning nor end. Everything is Here and Now. No beginning nor end. Everything is Here and Now. No beginning nor end. Everything is Here and Now. No beginning nor end. Everything is Here and Now No beginning nor end. Everything is Here and Now. No beginning nor end. Everything is Here and Now. No beginning nor end. Everything is Here and Now. No beginning nor end. Everything is Here and Now. No beginning nor end. Everything is Here and Now. No beginning nor end. Everything is Here and Now. No beginning nor end. Everything is Here and Now. No beginning nor end. Everything is Here and Now.

Other publications by the same author:

How to become a christ: A method in forthy days!
— BOD Editions

Jack the Ripper is not a man
— Amazon Editions